SPOTS

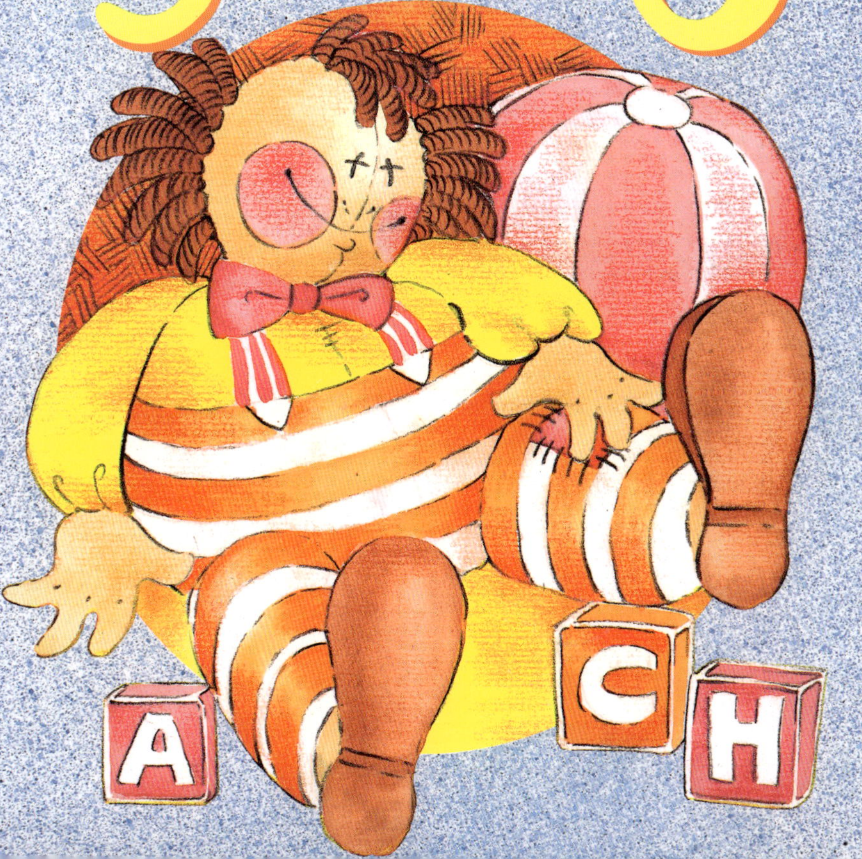

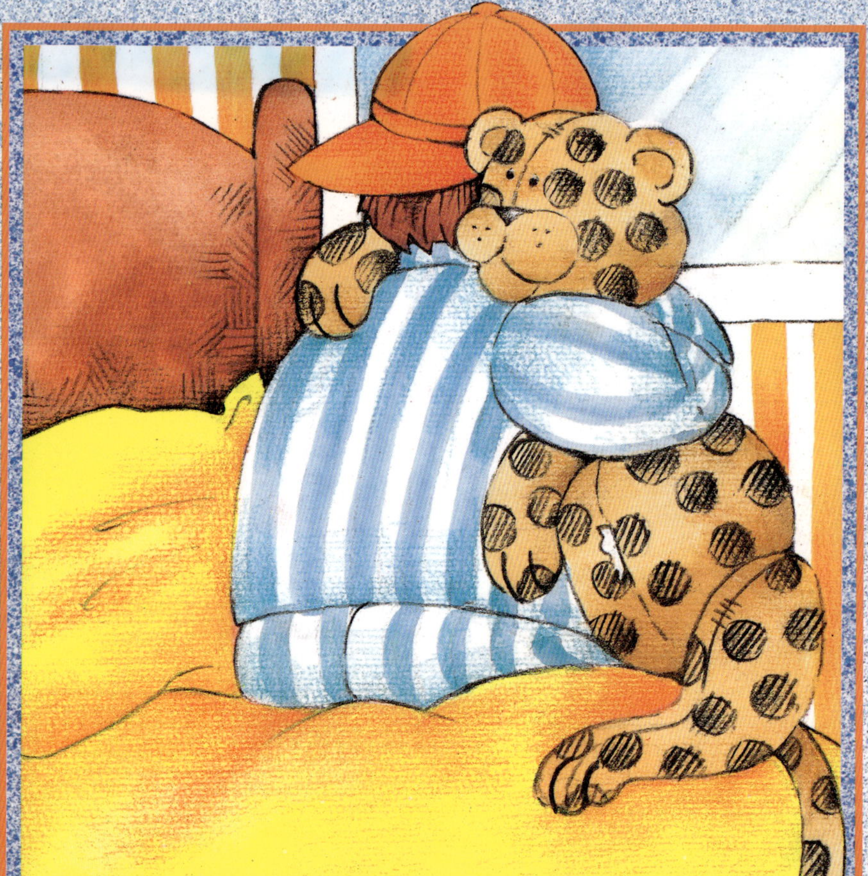

My leopard has spots
down to his toes.

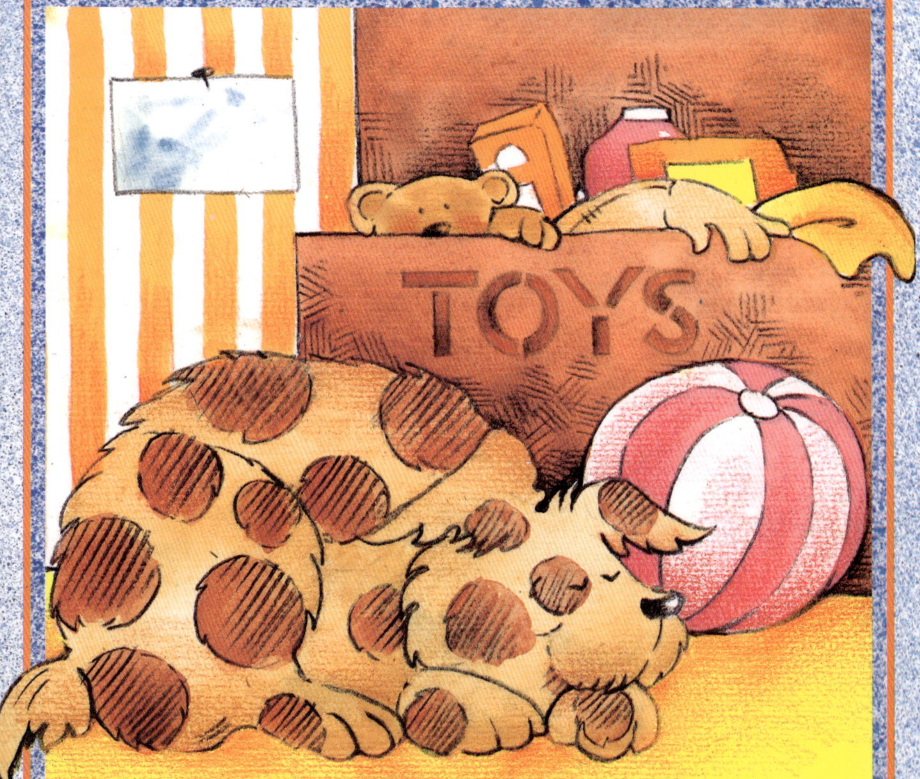

My dog has spots
except on his nose.

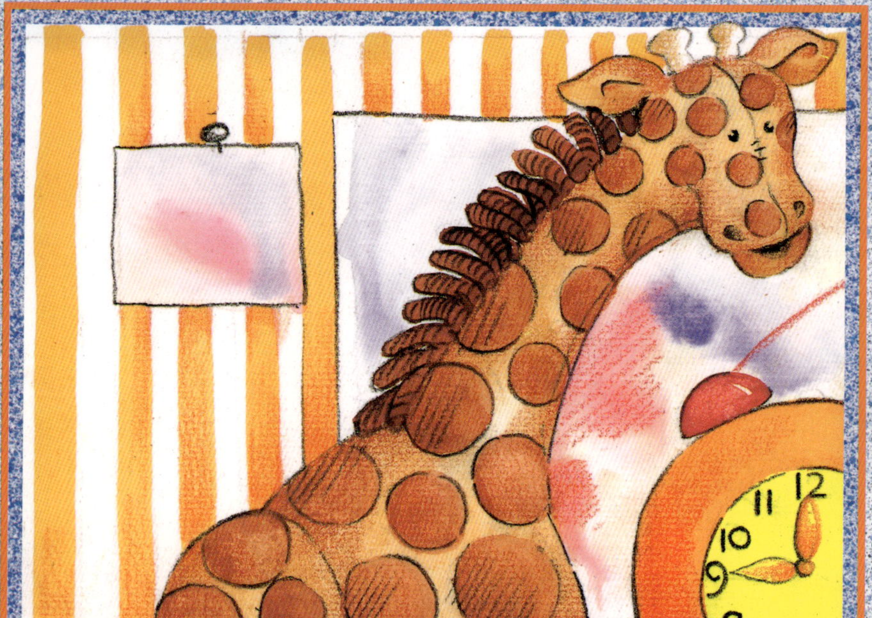

My giraffe has spots
all over the place.

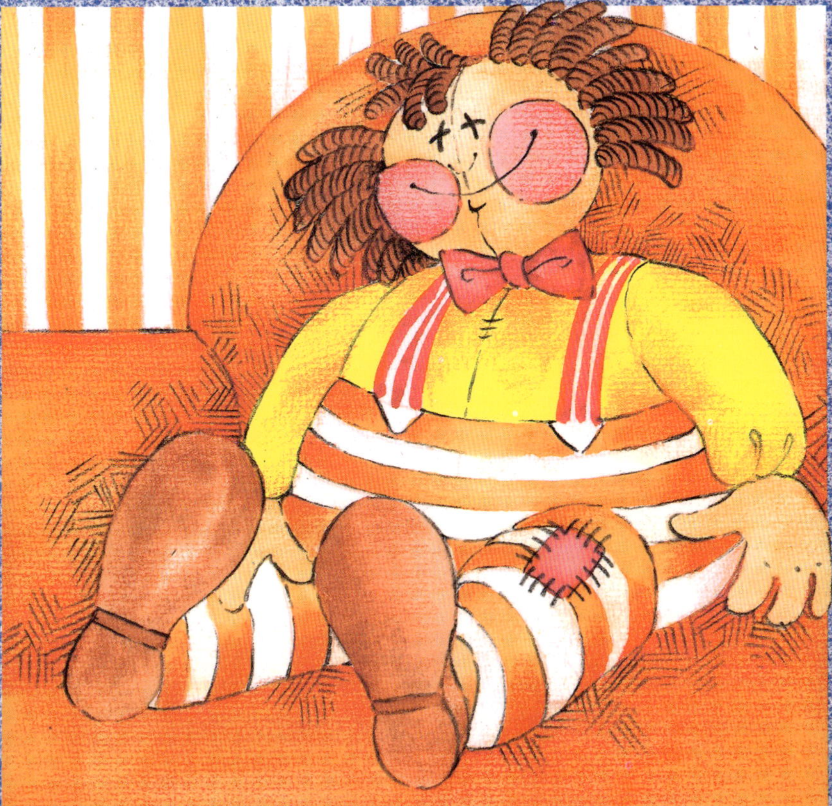

My clown has two
big spots on his face.

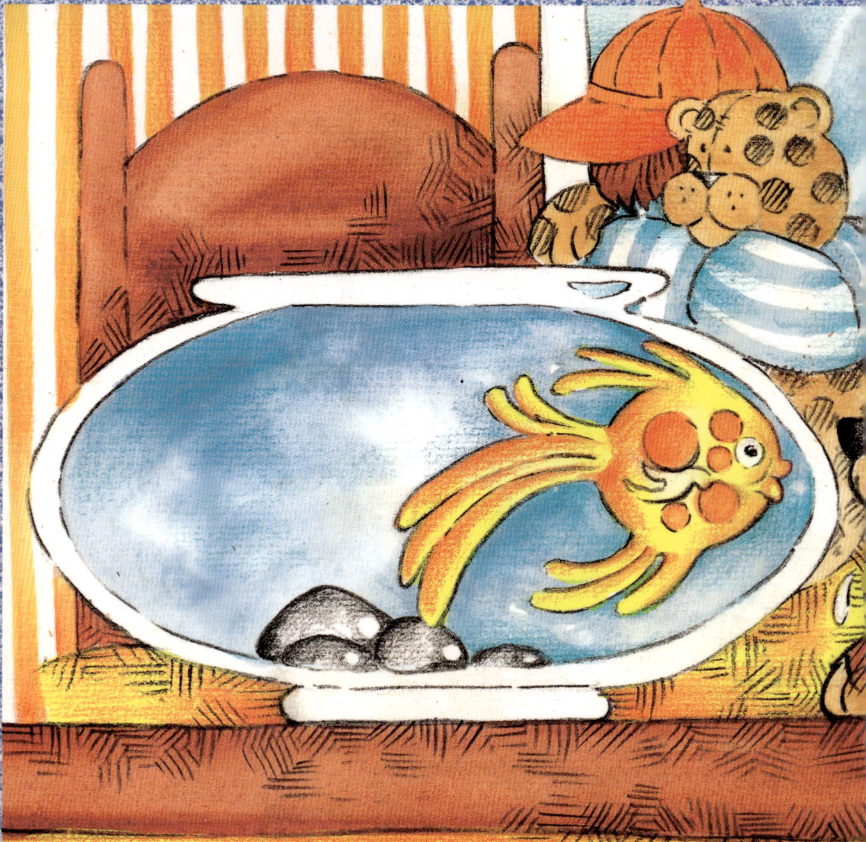

My fish has a few spots
here and there.

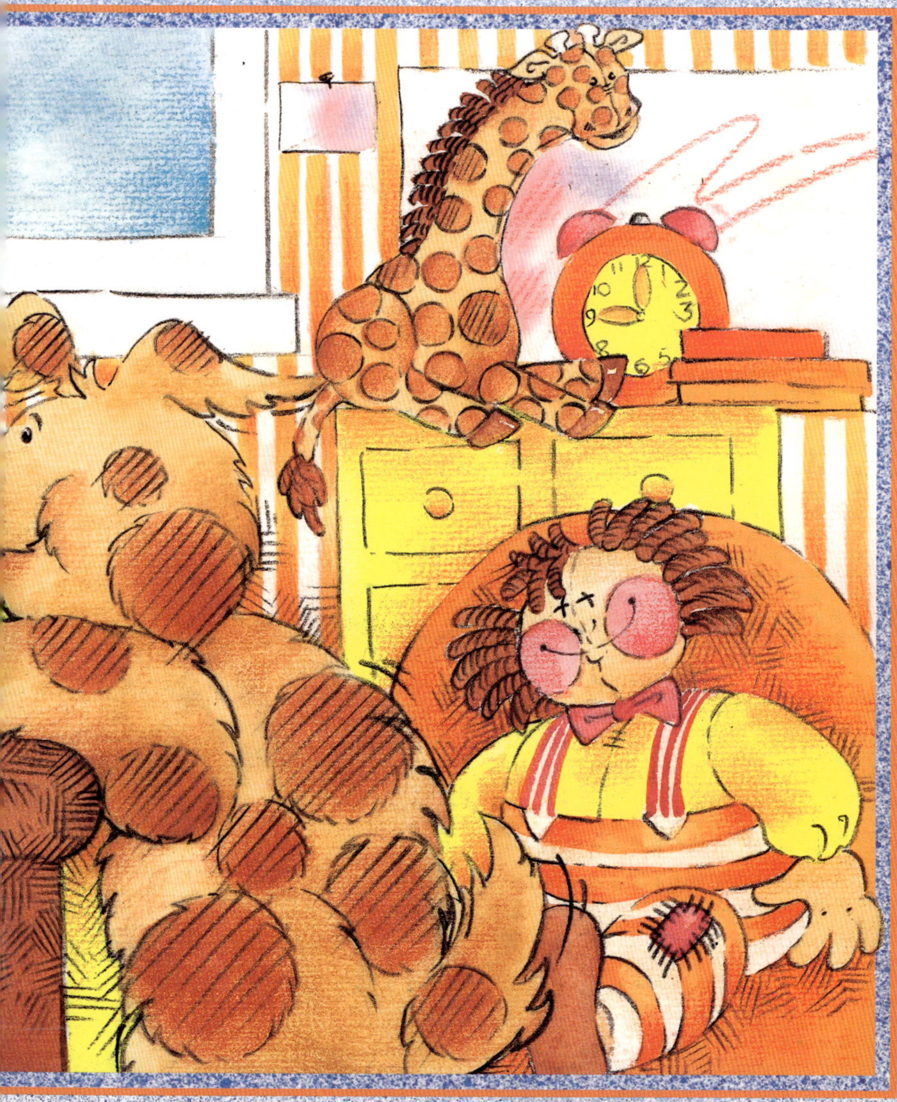

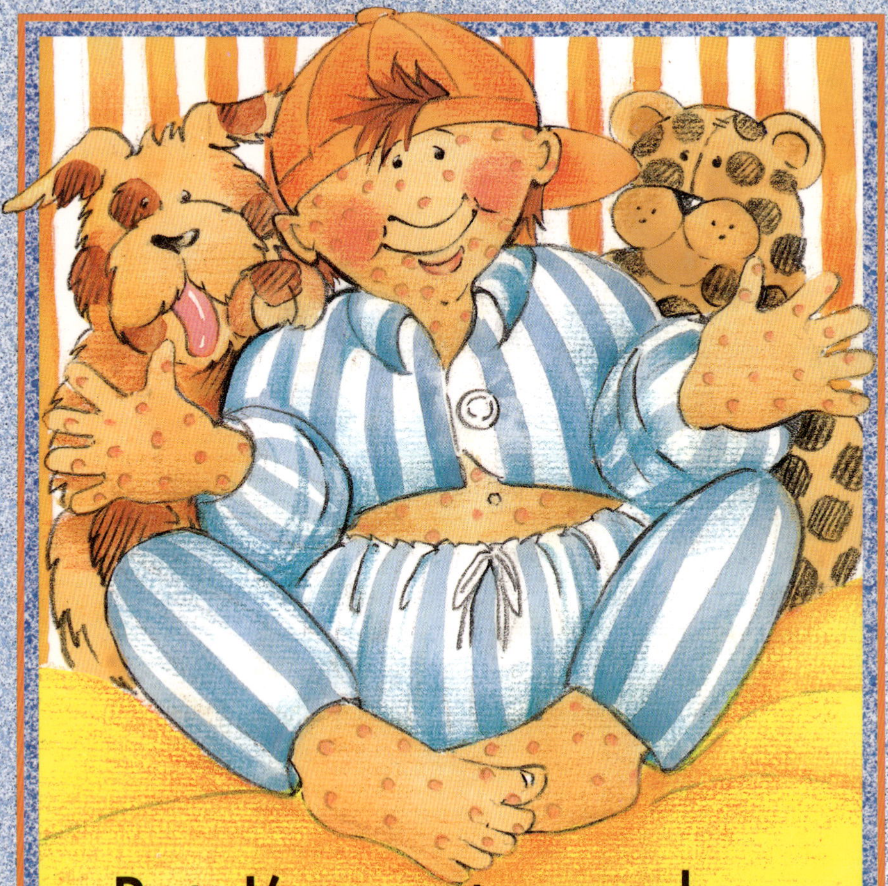

But I've got measle
spots EVERYWHERE!